A Journey *of* Recovery

A Memoir by

STEPHEN MULLEN

PAGE PUBLISHING
Conneaut Lake, PA

First originally published by
Page Publishing 2024

ISBN 979-8-89315-967-7 (pbk)
ISBN 979-8-89315-986-8 (digital)

Printed in the United States of America

I came home from school thinking everyone was saying that I had a "big nose" under their breath. It really bothered me, and I began to think that I did indeed have a big nose when all this time, I was happy with my physical appearance until then. Hearing that I had a "big nose" was an auditory hallucination because, in reality, no one ever said such a thing. Anyway, I went on with my life for a few weeks, even forgetting what I had heard about my nose being big, until I started "hearing" voices once again.

"I have been raped and drugged," I yelled out in the middle of the night on a dead-end street.

The next morning, I found a note left by my mother saying, "Steve, you are on drugs and are no longer welcome in this house."

She was partly right—I was smoking strong weed at the time, and I believed that smoking weed at an early age ignited an early onset of mental illness. I called my dad and asked if I could live with him for the meanwhile, and he welcomed me into his house with open arms.

My dad lived in a large Victorian-style house in Boston that was built in the 1800s. I was so excited about living with my dad, seeing how my parents divorced when I was just an adolescent. My dad had many rooms with old oak wooden floors that I absolutely fell in love with as a kid when visiting his house. My dad had an exercise room, which I took advantage of! I started lifting weights and hitting the punching bag, which gave me relief in meditating my mind from the "voices," even though I was not yet fully aware that I was even hearing voices.

Everything was going well at my dad's house until I decided to smoke some weed I had brought with me. "I am going to poison Steve in his sleep tonight," I swore I heard my father say to his friend during a phone call. So I ran out of the house to dial 911. The neighbors did indeed call the police, and they came. The authorities were aware that I was mentally unwell, and the next thing I knew, I was being taken to the nearby hospital. My family visited me, and they tried to bring me home, but my trust in my family, never mind anyone at all, had vanished for the time being.

After a few days in the hospital, I was driven in an ambulance to an inner-city mental hospital. The appearance of the facility was prison-like, making me want to burst into tears. I asked myself, "Why am I being punished for doing nothing wrong?" I soon came to find out that there was a mix of both kind and dangerous souls. I lay in my room for a week, thinking about possibly missing high school graduation, never mind graduation itself, because I had a court date soon so I could get the hell out of here, I so thought. Finally, the court date came to fruition, and I was asked to speak on the stand. When on the stand, I went into a psychosis, stating how I had suspicions about my family and believed I had been drugged and raped. Fortunately, to my benefit, I was obviously not released that day from the mental hospital, but I was sentenced to just a month in the mental hospital instead.

During my stay in my first mental facility, I would sometimes hear the fellow patients linger around the door to my room in the middle of the night. I am not certain whether it was out of paranoia connected to the hallucinations I was experiencing, but I strongly believed that my life was at risk. One day, I decided to take pencils out of the art room and place them under my thin mattress. I did not want to use them, but I was ready to use them in self-defense for my life. The staff did eventually notice the pencils and took them from under my mattress, but nothing was ever said to me.

There was a group session during the day, but my paranoia and fear for my life caused me to sleep in the daytime, even though there were emotions and issues I needed to address in the therapy sessions. One night in the hospital, I had a dream in which some of the patients gathered around my room to beat me to death, but I pleaded for my life, and they left. The next night, I had the same dream, but this time the patients came to kill me. However, two twin angels of light led me out of the mental hospital with their shining silver swords. Although it was just a dream, I still believe that it was a sign from God to continue my life's journey toward the path of Good as both a survivor and a fighter.

Having this dream filled with the presence of angels caused a rebirth in me. I felt as though God took away all my talents and gifts, and I had to start anew at the age of nineteen. Even though my natural-born gifts had departed from me, I believe I was gifted with the potential to do anything I wanted. So I contemplated during these long days in the mental hospital, while sitting on my hospital bed, about what I was going to do in life now that I was a "changed" person. I figured out that I had to better myself in life by continuing what I was doing—playing sports and building wisdom—but with a whole new outlook, because I feel to this day that my mind had been replaced by God or another higher being.

Often, I would be asked by a few other patients about when I was going to be released. I never responded because I knew better. One day, I was tearing up while sitting in a chair in the hallway when a staff lady I had never noticed before came up to me and said, "No one cares about you in here. This is the next step toward prison." I found these words harsh but honest, and I became enlightened to the fact that I was on the path toward prison, even though this dangerous mental illness was by no means my fault. A diagnosis was found for my mental illness; the doctors diagnosed me with bipolar disorder. I never mentioned to anyone about hearing "voices" since realizing it in the mental hospital, and for that, I regret it. Bipolar disorder was a misdiagnosis because I wasn't fully honest with the doctor; I thought I would never be released if I admitted to auditory hallucinations. I was eventually released and went home to a safer place, my dad's house. Although I was overjoyed about regaining my freedom, losing my freedom at such a young age traumatized my mind because I felt as though my first mental hospital, especially, was an experience of torture.

I missed my last month of high school, but the dean of my school, also my friend, allowed me to graduate. I had planned on studying abroad in Spain at a university I had been accepted to, but those plans were wiped away because I was in no state of mind to go to college, never mind studying abroad, even though I was one of the few selected for this overseas educational experience. I was not the same person anymore because my life's work was now focused on mental recovery. However, I do feel that becoming ill when I did was almost a blessing in disguise because I would not have wanted to have a mental breakdown in another country, like Spain.

I sure thought that this would be my last hospitalization, but boy, was I wrong! This was just the beginning of a long and continuous journey in dealing with an inner demon of life—schizophrenia. I would have long conversations with my dad every day, and he would inform me about the news in the world, especially around Boston. The medicine slowed down my mind drastically, and it felt like my intelligence and talents had been depleted or taken away. I do believe my dad noticed the slowness of my mentality, and through conversations of wisdom, he solved the issue. It became clear to me that my dad's mission was to bring forth mental healing in me, even though he worked a good but hard job. For a long time, it felt like I would never leave this "pretty penny" of a house because my dad's house was a place of sanctuary where we played ping pong and watched movies, among other things.

My dad and I would play catch and basketball at the park in South Boston. We would often get burgers and fries at the beachside, where we sat on a bench and ate while looking at the ocean. The times shared with my dad were priceless, advancing me forward in life because I had a best friend. Although I left my friends and acquaintances behind, I was happy in life with my dad.

I didn't see my mom for almost a year after my first hospitalization, out of choice, because of mistrust. But my mom was relentless in looking out for my safety and well-being. She would sometimes leave food at the front door because I wouldn't answer the phone. I eventually regained a strong relationship with my mom, as she supported me with life experiences. She would take me throughout many parts of New Hampshire during my recovery from mental illness. My mom and I would fish for trout in the streams and splash each other with water, which triggered youth and happiness in me.

My mom is a yoga and Qigong teacher, among other holistic offerings she possesses. I mention my mom's profession because her teaching of meditation and peace was crucial in my recovery from mental illness. I was provided with techniques for protecting myself energetically as well as sending out positive energy. I learned how to "play" with energy because my mom informed me, based on her beliefs, that I was being attacked energetically. So I acquired meditation skills in the holistic arts, learning how to shield myself from energy filled with evil intent. I was a well-known kid growing up, athletic and smart. However, jealousy is an evil that exists, and I quickly came to learn that not everyone liked me, even though I always tried to exude kindness to all individuals. I also found out that once I became ill and was no longer the same outgoing person, people forgot about me rather quickly. However, I realized that my family, the ones who supported me, were all I needed in life during this time.

I stopped speaking to my friends because I believed I was a joke to them all this time because when I was down in the dumps, no one cared but a few people. I soon came to realize that when I was hanging out with my so-called friends, I forgot who my true friends were—my family. My granny would cook a couple of meals a week for me and my dad, and to be honest, her meals were like no other, as she cooked delicious Italian cuisines. I was also very close to my grandad, who was a hardworking, honest, and admirable man, and I felt so proud to have him as one of my best friends! I loved watching movies with my grandparents and conversing with them because they were such interesting people who had seen and been through so much in history. Feeling comfortable around my family was not an issue because no one was judging me. My other grandparents on my mother's side were also my mentors, especially through the talks regarding life's wisdom and Christianity we shared. They healed me mentally because I needed their love. I mention the non-judgment of my grandparents because I felt judged by the world, as I had a few sexual experiences with another male who came on to me when I was young. I know there is nothing wrong with homosexuality, but having homosexual experiences and being judged for it when all this time I thought of myself as a heterosexual male brought me nearer to suicide.

There were times when I would envision myself hanging from a rope in my dad's attic. I also felt a constant weight as if I had chains on my legs, which lingered in me for years. My brother, however, lifted this weight off my body through therapy by talking about what was troubling my mind. Once becoming mentally ill, I became aware out of common sense that my experience with another male was known by others. I had many other issues I regretted because I was hearing "insulting" voices that were both judging me and watching my every move. I learned not to care what people think, and I became filled with more self-acceptance every day, which brought me closer to God because I needed His strength to continue my path in life toward recovery.

My grandparents on my mother's side were very holy and religious, and I must believe their prayers gave me courage and guidance to not only live a good life but also to shine my light in the world from the gifts God gave me. Prayer is a form of energy, and we as humans are recipients of energy, whether good or bad. So I started to pray to

God for help, and my prayers were answered through the eyes of my family, who were watching over me. My brother would also cleanse the energy in the house with crystals, as it is believed by many that crystals possess healing and protective qualities. I came to know that these crystals do indeed have their own form of intelligence because I could feel the negative energy being repelled by these crystals during the night.

The nightmares I had were true terrors, which sometimes made me believe these nightmares did indeed occur. For example, one night I dreamt that I was raped by my dog, with my mom's approval. I had many other horrible dreams, such as being drugged and having my tongue cut. Clearly, these nightmares were not real, but the vivid dreaming experience caused these dreams to seem quite real. I ended up being hospitalized repeatedly because these visual and auditory hallucinations were triggering psychosis after psychosis. I was admitted to several more mental hospitals after my initial hospitalization, and I handled these hospitals fine.

My second hospitalization was at another inner-city mental hospital. Honestly, I say this with no racism, but I was the only white male in this mental hospital. However, even though I stuck out like a sore thumb, the people were quite nice! I apparently took too long of showers and used up all the hot water at times, but other than that, I rested and ate well there. Unfortunately, I do remember yelling out that I got raped by a dog as I awoke from a nightmare. My mom visited me and even left a photo album with some baked goods, but I threw them away in the trash because I was in a psychosis from lucid dreaming. I kept my feelings to myself, even though not sharing symptoms of my mental illness with the doctors was detrimental to me because I wasn't sleeping well anymore.

After only a few days at home after being hospitalized a second time, I was on my way to yet another mental facility. There was a little weed in the guest room at my dad's house, and I decided to smoke it. I had gone so long without smoking, but my addiction got the best of me. After smoking, I thought I had to barricade my room so I wouldn't be killed or raped. So I took all my belongings and furniture and placed them in front of the two entering doors to my room. I stayed up the entire night by my windows, making sure no one climbed a ladder to drug and torture me. The next day, my dad tried to give me my medicine, but he soon found out that he couldn't get into my room. He didn't know what to do, so he called my mom, and she called the police. "The angels will come," I yelled at the police as they forcefully tried to enter my bedroom. I do slightly remember swinging a bat at the door to frighten them away, but then I sat down on my bed as I was placed in cuffs. However, the authorities were good and decent people who saw a struggling human being, and I was driven to a mental hospital instead of jail. Once arriving at the mental hospital, my handcuffs were taken off, but sedating medication had entered my bloodstream. I was soon on my way to my third mental hospital.

At my third mental hospital, I finally felt comfortable enough to explain what was really going on with me. "I am hearing voices constantly and feel like I am going crazy," I told the doctor. Finally, medicine was found that reduced the hallucinations and made me feel safe enough to sleep in the mental hospital. One day, I hallucinated circles of blood on one of the older patients. I started to think that some of the patients were undergoing surgery, and I thought I was next to have my head cut open. I was, however, able to quickly overcome this psychosis by reaching reality once again. I spent a few months at this mental hospital, and I was not being let out even though there was no provocation for doing so. So I got a lawyer and went to court to at least fight to be released. In court, the doctor made up lies about my behavior, and when it was my time to speak, I confronted the doctor on his lies. The doctor was baffled, and the judge saw that I was doing much better mentally than when I was first admitted. I was released that very day and went home to my dad's house in Dorchester. Fortunately, I finally received a proper diagnosis for my mental illness and was informed that I suffer from schizophrenia.

I went to another mental hospital for a short while before being drugged out of my mind at my fifth mental institution. I recall being so dizzy from the medicine prescribed to me that I could barely make it to the hospital bed without falling to the ground. The medicine the staff was feeding me was heightening the hallucinations, making me forget the days and how long I had been hospitalized. There were days when I would wake up out of my sleep and then be punched in the face by a patient. I was punched multiple times, but sometimes I wasn't so drugged, and I wrestled a person or two to the ground. Violence really wasn't my thing, but I had to maintain a violent mind, I thought anyway, to survive this mental hospital. Sometimes I would hallucinate "little people" dancing around my head as I tried to sleep. I really don't know what drugs I was on, but I was aware that I was "tripping." After three months at this mental facility, I was released to my home with Dad!

My dad and I had a close relationship. I had lived with him for six years, and although we were making slow but solid progress, it was progress nonetheless toward the advancement of my mental healing. Unfortunately, the last time that I was properly medicated was when I was at my third mental hospital. The therapists and doctors I saw outside of the mental facilities were no help. It is not that they didn't care, but schizophrenia is an illness that is nowhere near being understood. My blood was taken often to test my blood levels from the medicine prescribed to me. There were even times I needed to have my blood taken weekly because one of the side effects of the medicine was sudden death. A change of environment was needed, so I decided to leave the city for a while.

I moved with my mom to New Hampshire, and initially, things were going great at my mom's house. My mom and her husband Larry, since childhood, had built and cleared the land for an estate in the middle of the forest in the mountains of New Hampshire. As a kid, there was just a small wooden cottage where my brothers and I used to stay before the house was built and the land was cleared. I was staying in the guest suite part of the house, which had a full bathroom, a bedroom, and a grand room with a fireplace and surrounding glass doors known as a sunroom. One day, I started projecting angelic as well as demonic chants because I didn't think anyone heard them. However, someone did hear me chanting, and they didn't like it, so they called the authorities. Suddenly, multiple ambulances and police cars came to my mom's house. "Can I smoke a cigarette before you take me?" I asked the officer, and he let me. I found myself being taken to yet another hospital for observation. I admitted to hallucinating and was released but provided with a therapist and doctor in the state of New Hampshire due to my mental condition. I returned to my mom's house for the meantime, and without knowing it, I was on the path toward recovery. I met a doctor who found the proper medication for me. I was finally sleeping soundly through the night again, and the hallucinations dwindled.

There was a rock in my mom's yard where I could play wall-ball with the lacrosse stick. My mom would take me to swimming holes where we would fish and swim with her sweetheart of a dog, Scarlett. My mom and I would go to many restaurants and venture through the state of New Hampshire. There were so many paths in the woods of New Hampshire that my mom, her dog Scarlett, and I took advantage of. Larry would have cookouts all the time, and I would eat like a king! I was used to eating plentifully anyway because my dad would buy and order copious amounts of food when we lived in Boston. I truly appreciated the hospitality of my mom and Larry, but what I most appreciated was becoming friends with Larry's father, Harry, especially since he had always looked out for my safety in these territorial parts of New Hampshire. I was ready, however, to go back home to Boston because I missed my dad and my American Bulldog, Thor.

Once again, I returned home, and my dad opened the doors to his house for me, no questions asked! Also, I was reunited with my beautiful and loving dog and brother, Thor. I started going on walks quite a bit with my dad, Thor, and my oldest brother, who liked visiting our house. We walked in the neighborhoods of Dorchester, which contain some houses with beautiful architecture of Victorian design. We also walked in the Blue Hills, where there were paths in the forests, and we would see snakes and other creatures that didn't belong in this Northern environment, including an anaconda that our dog, Thor, pounced on by a nearby swamp-like pond. Thor entering my life was a slice of heaven because I loved our walks of meditation, and it felt like just me, James, Thor, and Dad were the only people hiking in the woods of the Blue Hills at times. Shortly after being properly medicated, I applied to and was accepted at Southern New Hampshire University in an online program, where I am majoring in a career associated with English and Creative Writing.

I was doing great at SNHU, but I must admit I have had my hiccups. I was unfortunately admitted to a couple more mental hospitals while in school, causing me to withdraw from my courses at the time of institutionalization. Fortunately, I chose a university that is compassionate toward students with mental illnesses, while also offering never-ending wisdom gained in my courses associated with my major and other key knowledge of life gained. I ended up with an outstanding academic advisor who has guided me through much of the college process, and she has been instrumental in sustaining my dream of getting my bachelor's degree in the field of writing.

Reflect on my illness, I found out that schizophrenia isn't necessarily just a curse but also a gift also. The point is that since becoming diagnosed with schizophrenia, I became extremely sensitive to energy. I learned to shield myself from negative energy by utilizing holistic techniques of meditation learned from my brother and mom. Acquiring these skills of the holistic arts and utilizing them caused me to break through in life by reaching a state of happiness naturally once again rather than trying to achieve happiness. One of the gifts I feel in my rebirth of life after being diagnosed was reading energy, whether good or bad, while also picking up on different frequencies of energy, including the paranormal. For example, my dad's house was always rumored to be haunted, but I never experienced anything until I became schizophrenic. There were times when I was alone in my dad's house and I would hear the toilet flush upstairs, but I ignored it, not thinking too much of it. But one night I was lying in bed, and I heard footsteps coming to my room. However, once the spirit became aware that I heard it, it stopped walking, but then the footsteps started up again, coming even nearer to my room. I quickly rushed downstairs and slept on the couch with the lights on. Also, when I was living with my mom in New Hampshire, I saw a man on the side of the road who disappeared once I drove by him.

"Mom, I just hallucinated a man on the road."

"I saw him too," replied my mom.

Apparently, the locals of this town were aware of this spirit because Larry asked if he was wearing a green shirt, and he was. I found out that he used to do wood-cutting on the land I was living on, which I found more interesting than freaky. My illness helped validate a belief I held all my life: the existence of the afterlife. Besides being interested in a career revolving around the art of writing, I am also quite fascinated by the afterlife. Having my belief that there is a life beyond earth through validation of the paranormal brought me closer to God because I believe there is a place of paradise after this life for all deserving souls.

Schizophrenia has humbled me in many ways. I have come to accept myself and my imperfections, such as being a bisexual male.

I eventually came to find out that the only person who cares about my sexuality is me at this point in life. For a long time, I was disappointed with God for creating me this way because I never saw myself as anything but a heterosexual male. However, I learned to be honest with myself because I am now aware that I am a creature of God like all walks of life on Earth, and for that, I am grateful, even with my imperfections. I find closure in knowing that the only perfect being in this entire universe is God Himself because God can only judge me, and for that, I must trust in God.

I eventually moved to Southwest Florida with Thor and my dad. I love it here and believe I have found my former happy self once again! I am doing well with my courses and am getting that much nearer to gaining my bachelor's degree. I feel as though I have overcome schizophrenia by finally accepting my former non-acceptant self while also adjusting to the symptoms of schizophrenia by taking my medication along with other methods. May the guardian angels be with the tortured souls who have not yet fully recovered from schizophrenia as well as with the rest of humanity, as they were with me in a time of crisis.

About the Author

Stephen Mullen is a writer who attends an online program for a major in creative writing and English at Southern New Hampshire University. He is currently working with a publication coordinator at a full-service publishing house, Page Publishing, for the release of his memoir *A Journey of Recovery*. Stephen was initially intending to go to college after high school for a major in business; he was one of the selected few to study abroad in Spain. However, a serious mental illness—schizophrenia—halted those plans, but this diagnosis ended up being a blessing in disguise because it created an entirely new path in life for him—a path of writing. Stephen has gained much insight into mental illnesses through his adjustment to schizophrenia in life, which he reflects in his wisdom of mental health as symbolized through some of his stories. He writes short stories filled with horror and fantasy, as well as memoirs focusing on the challenges of mental illnesses. He plans on continuing to have his stories published once his first story has been officially published. Stephen is an inspiration for many, seeing how he proves that obstacles of life can be faced and defeated, such as how Stephen exemplifies the naturalness of resilience that we, as humans, have the capability to harness within as a means for surviving and moving forward from life's obstacles. He now resides in Southwest Florida, which he loves due to its tropical weather and beauty. However, he has recently lost his American Bulldog, Thor, but he remains strong because he has faith that he will reunite with Thor again in heaven.